THIS BOOK BELONGS TO

CHICKENS ROOSTERS
RABBITS & MORE

FARM ANIMAL COLORING BOOK
24 DESIGNS

Enjoy this wonderful collection of 24 Farm Animal designs that you will love coloring. Escape to a world of creative inspiration and joy. Chickens, Roosters, Rabbits and more await you at every turn of the page. We hope that our intricate line drawings will help generate quietness and wellness in your mind as you watch your creations come to life. Printed on one side only.

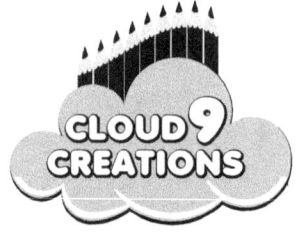

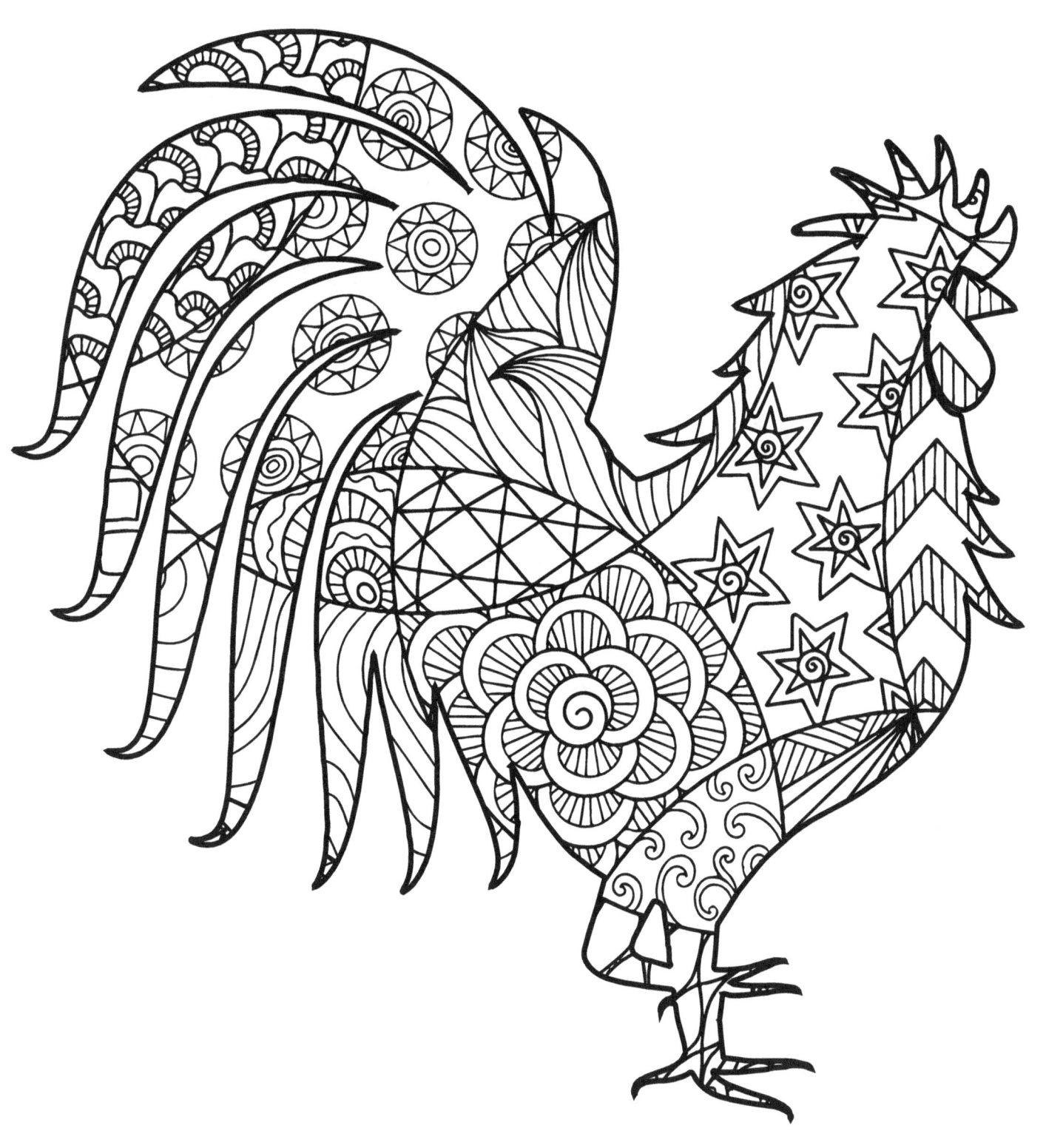

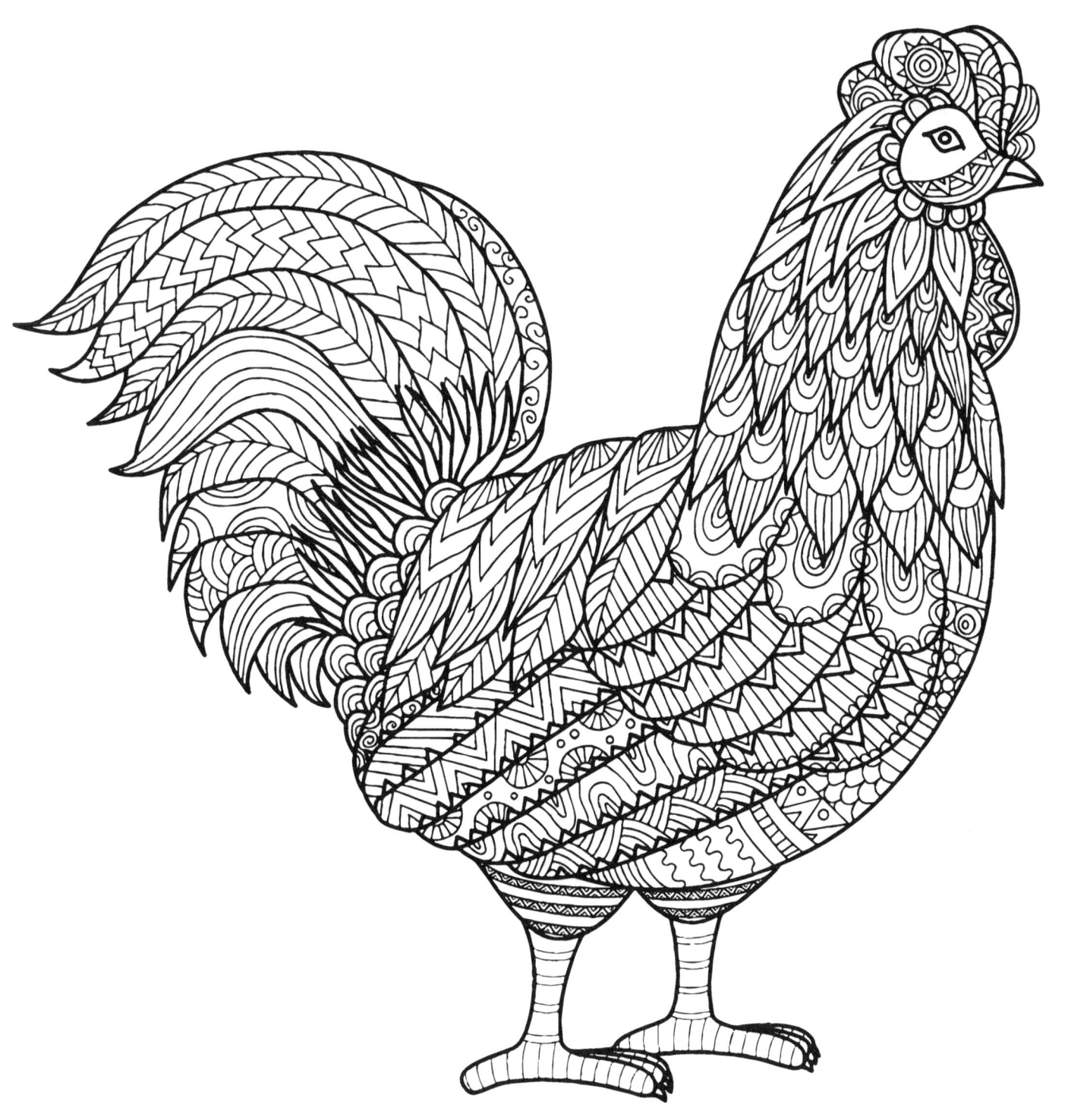

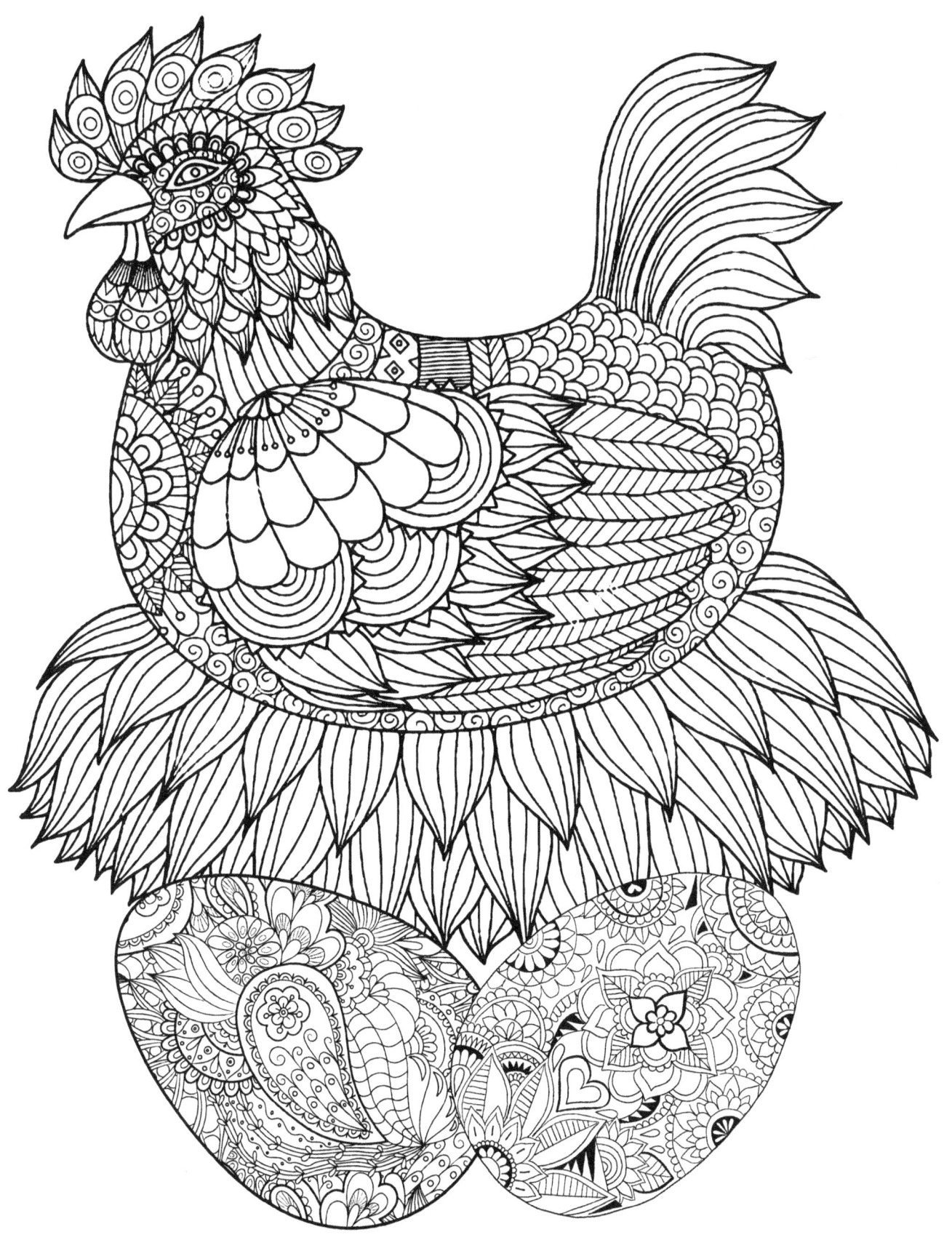

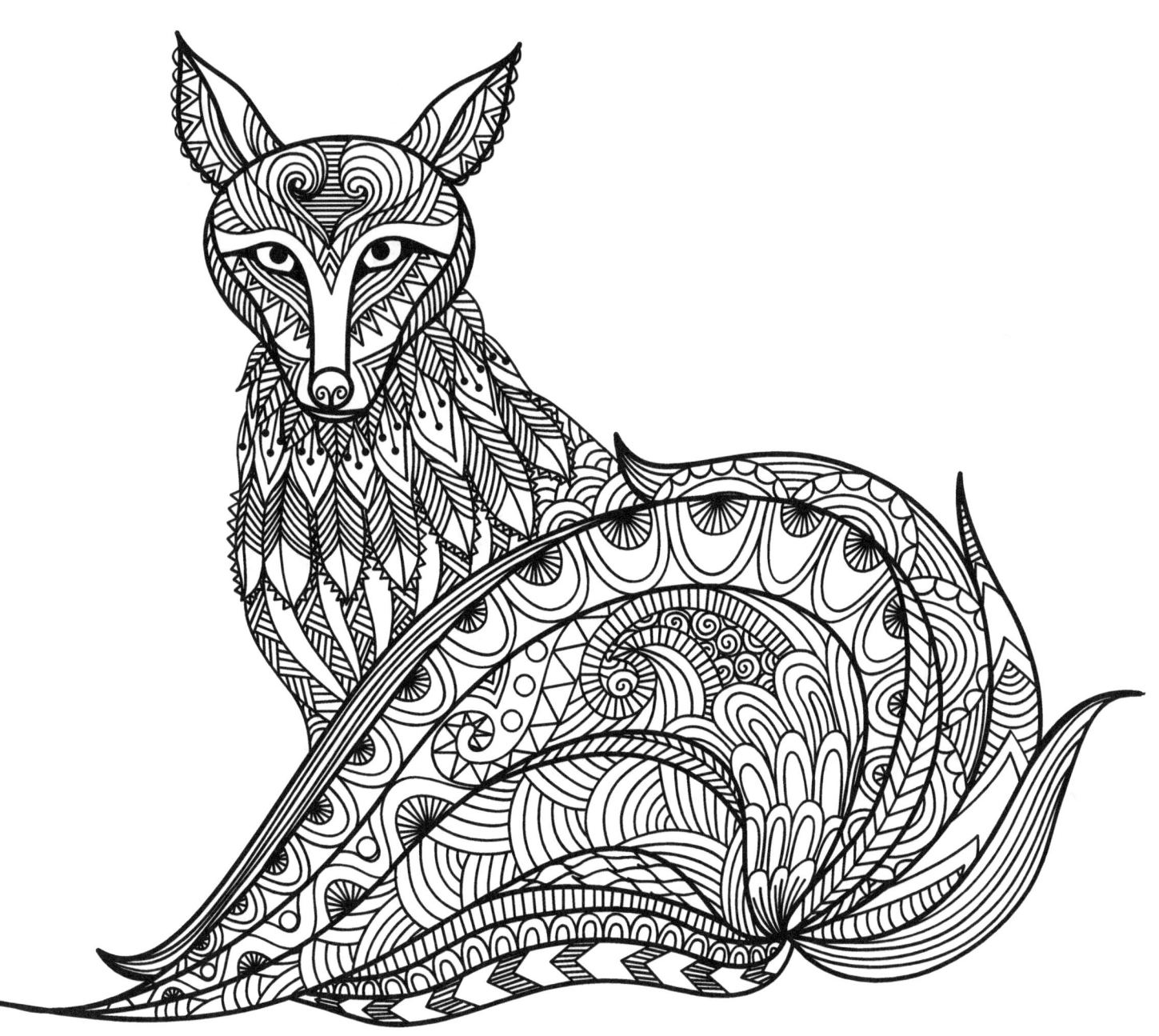

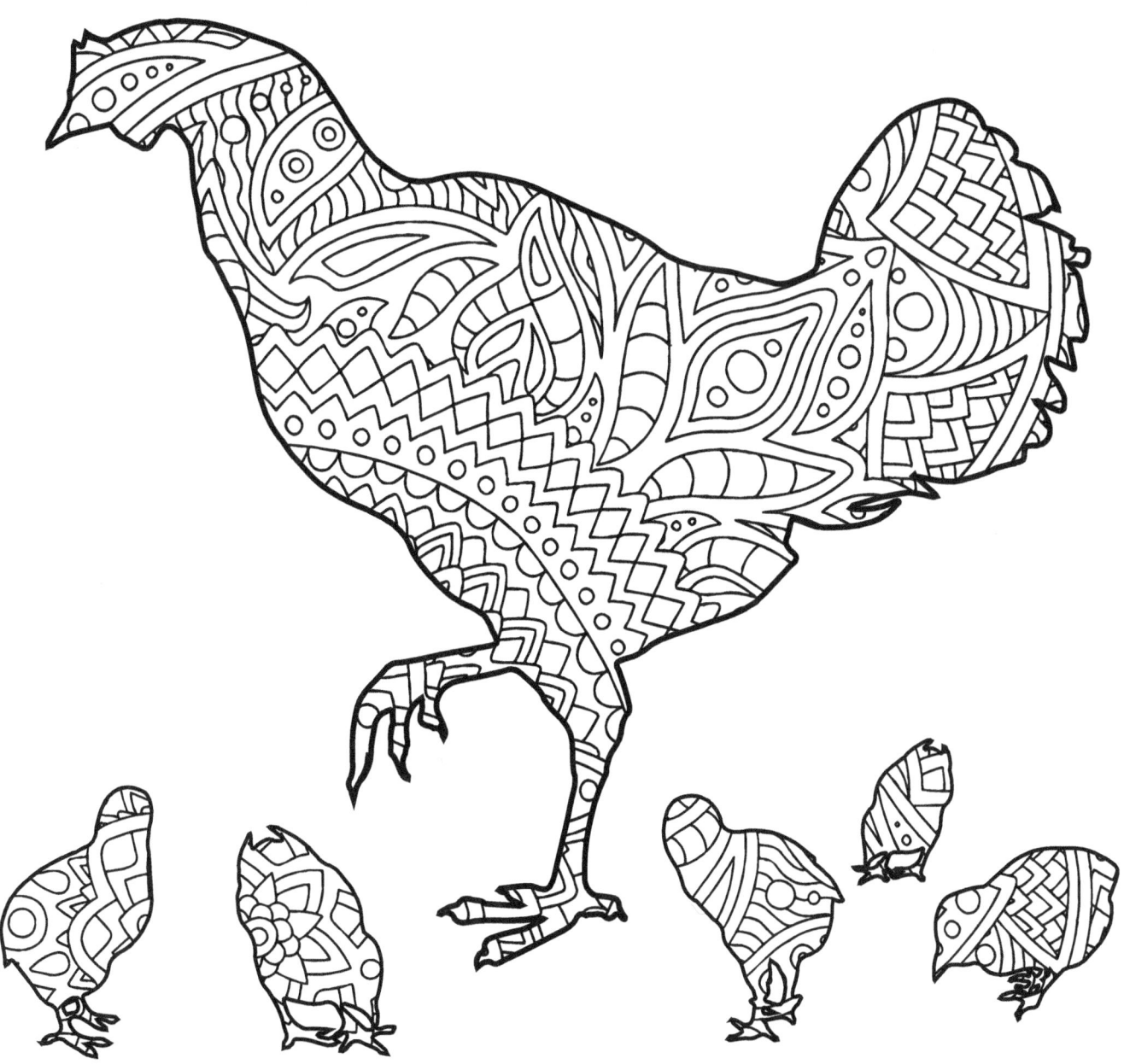

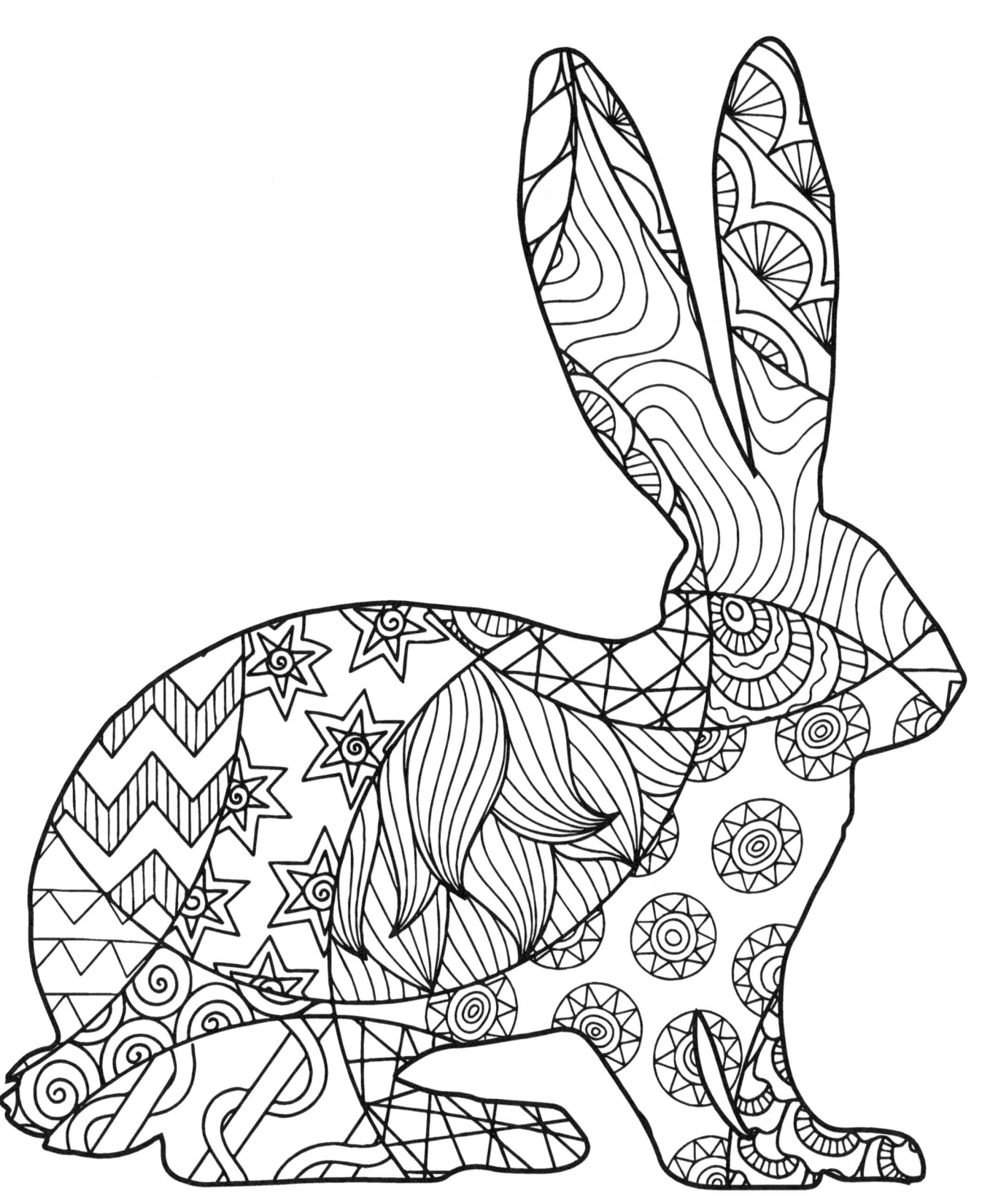

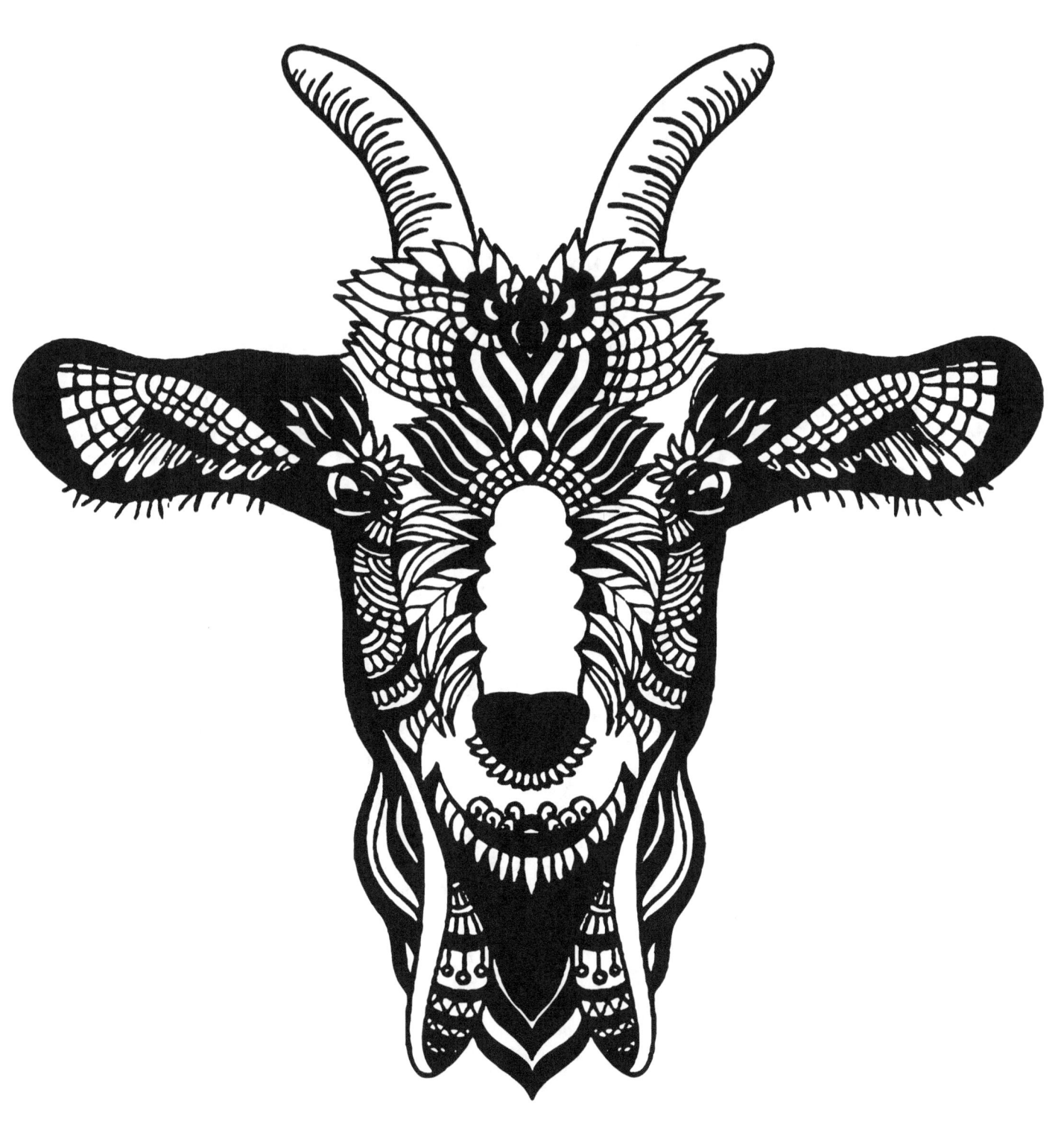

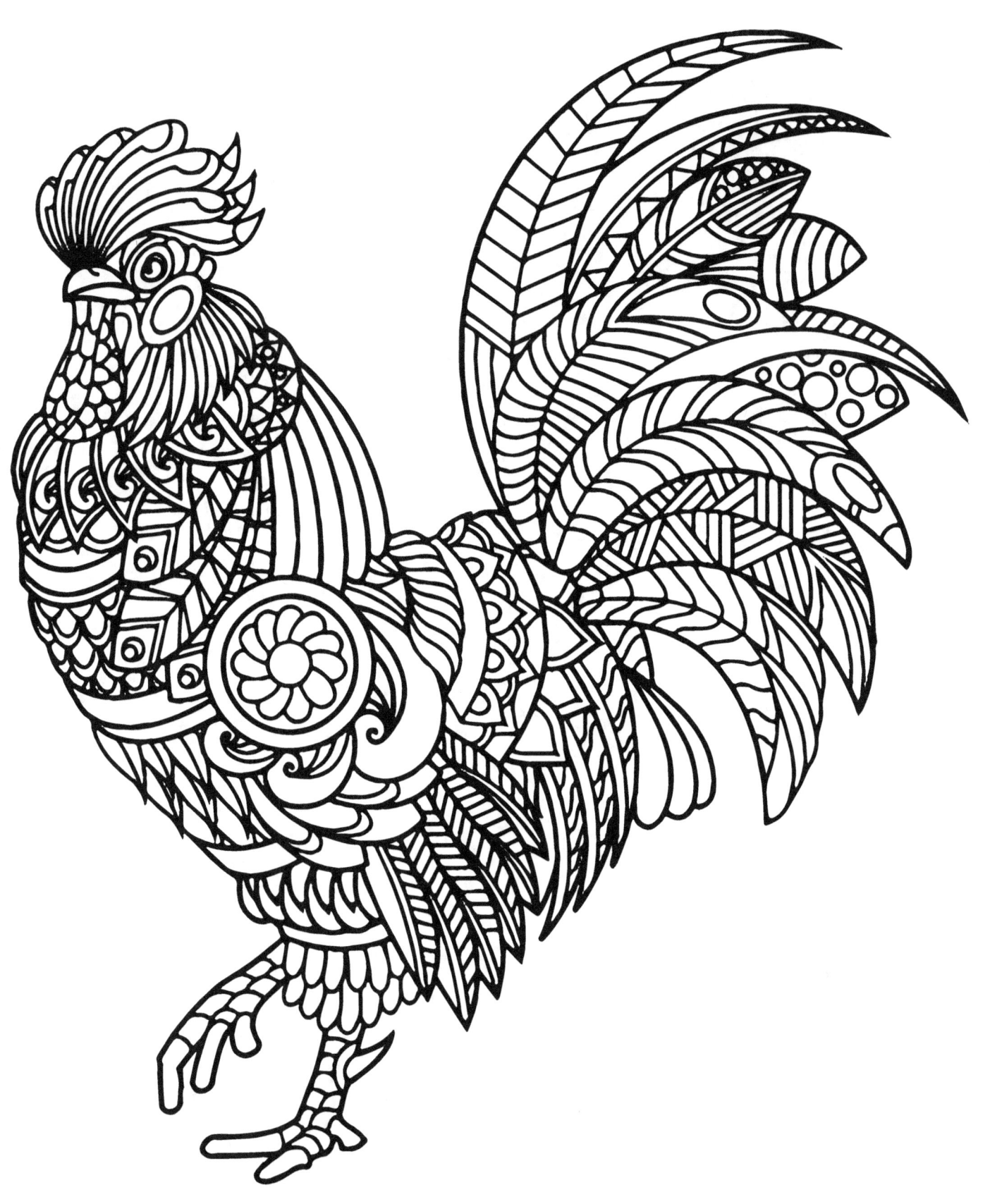

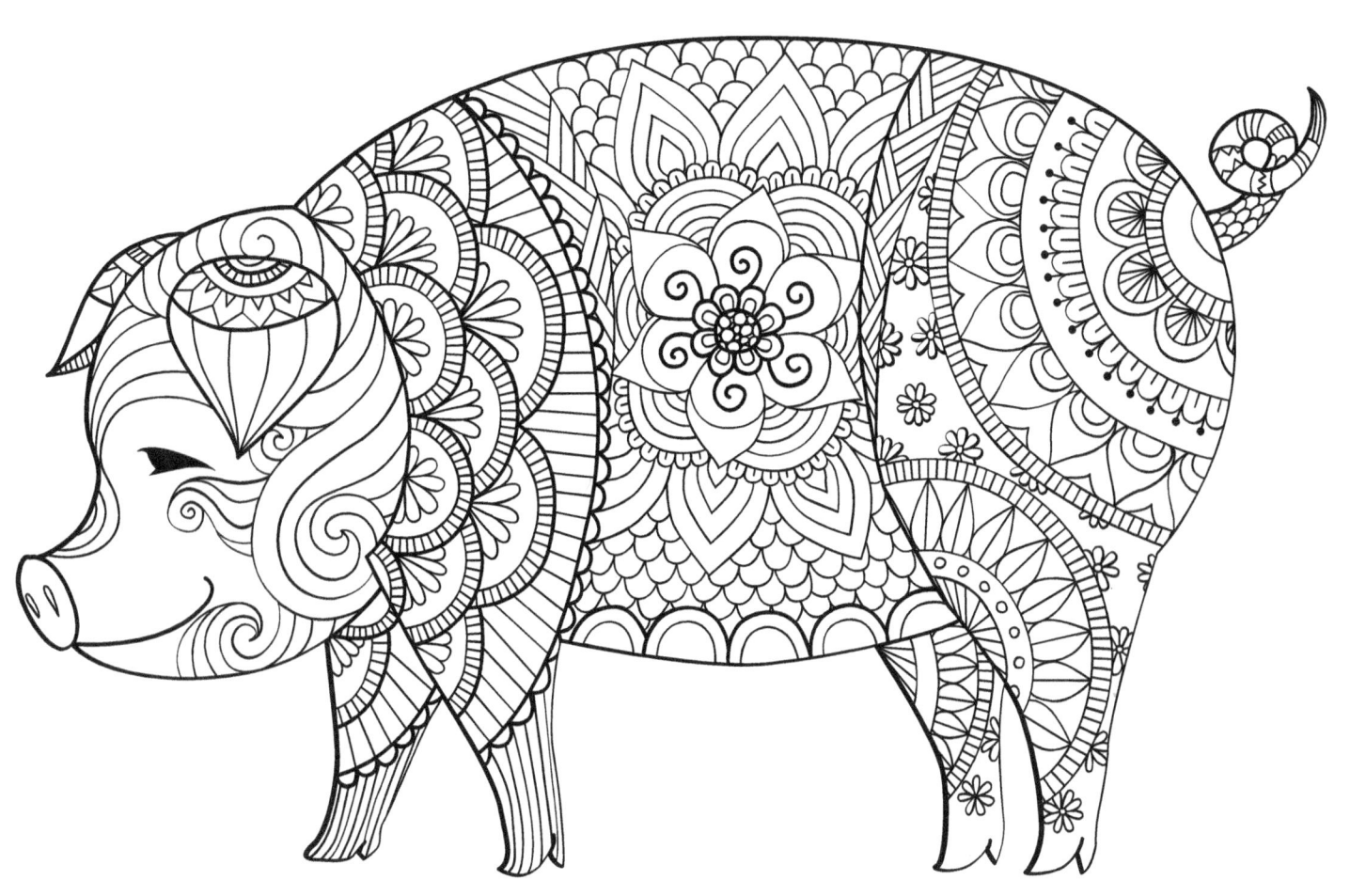

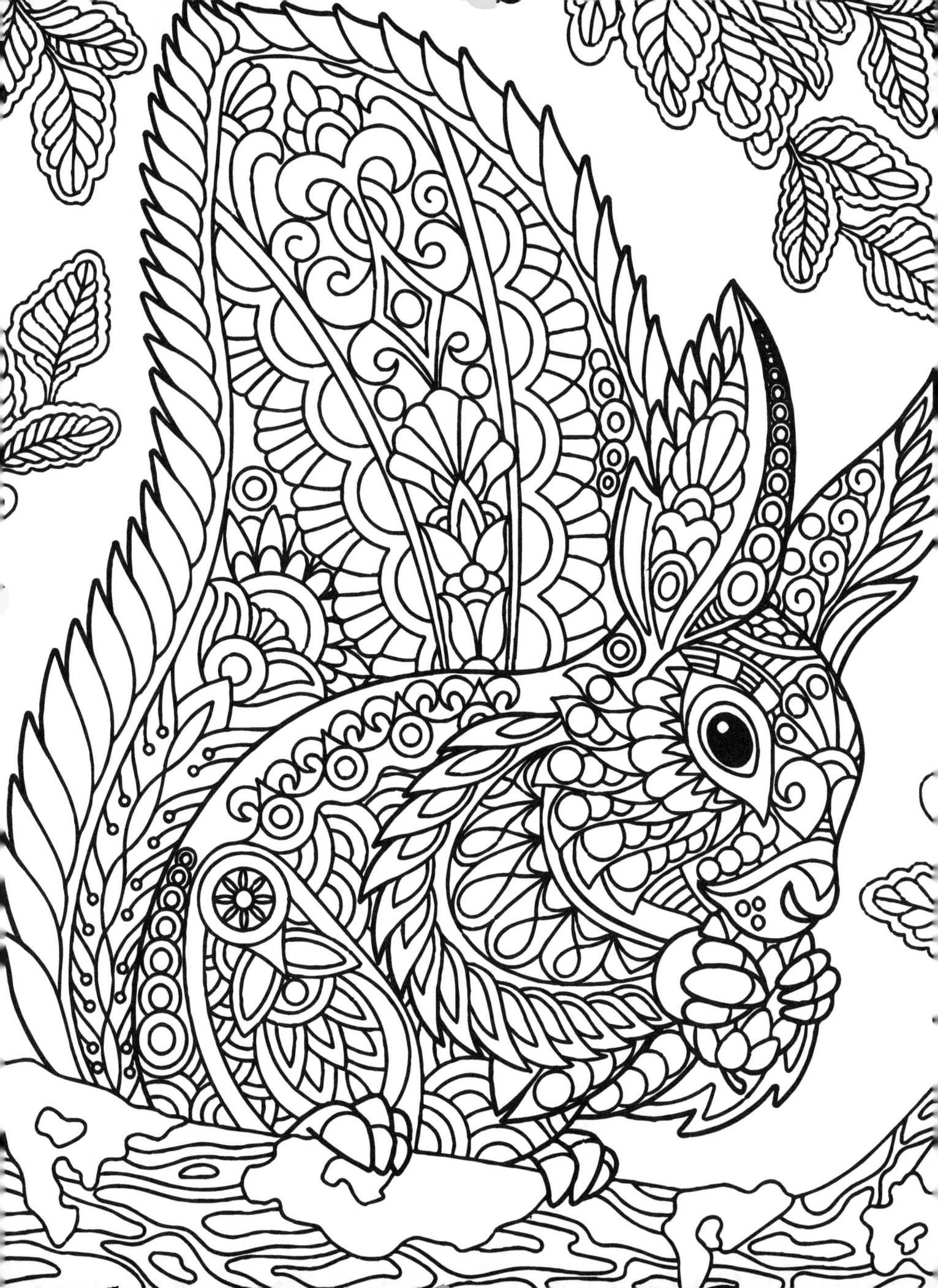

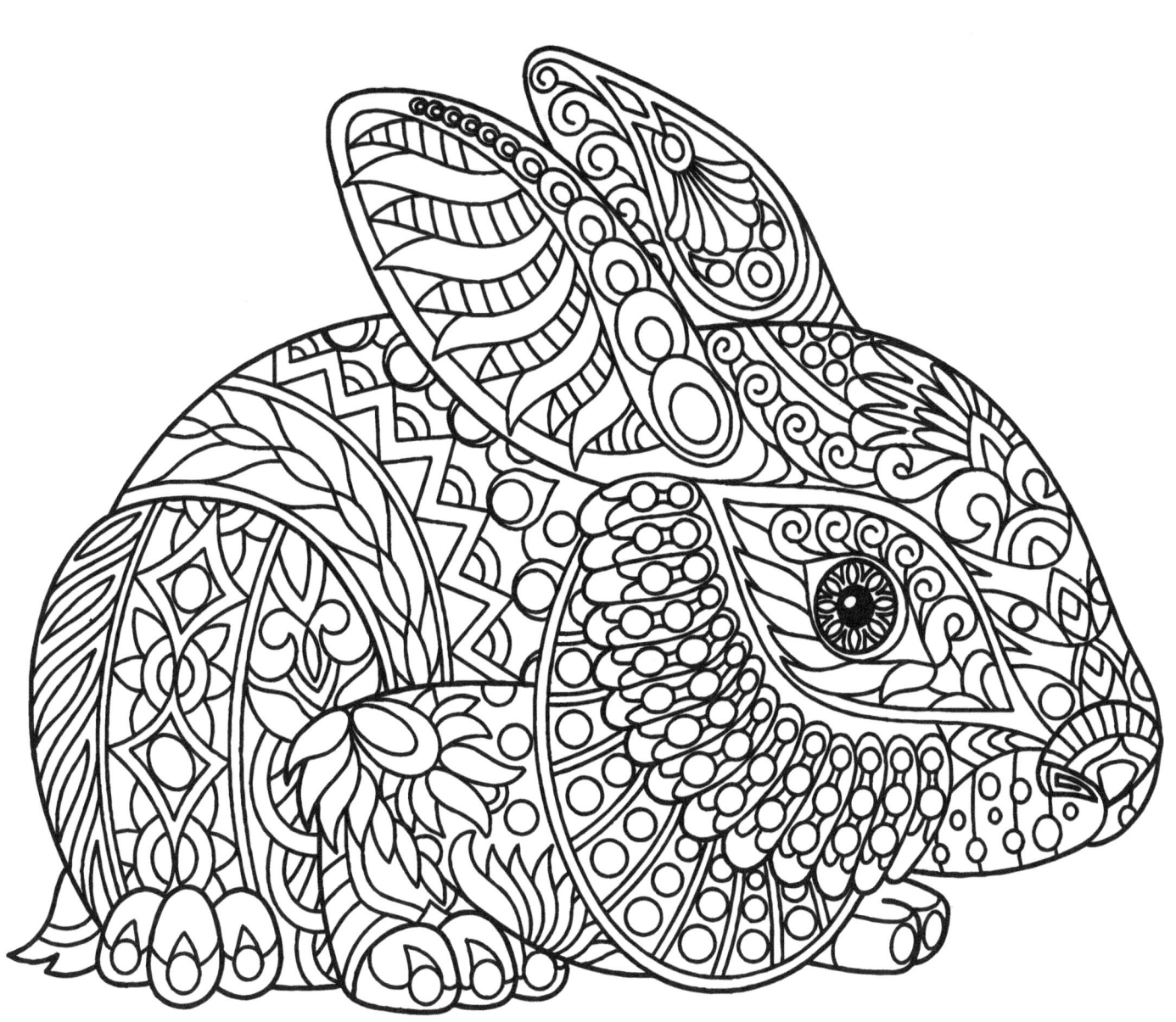

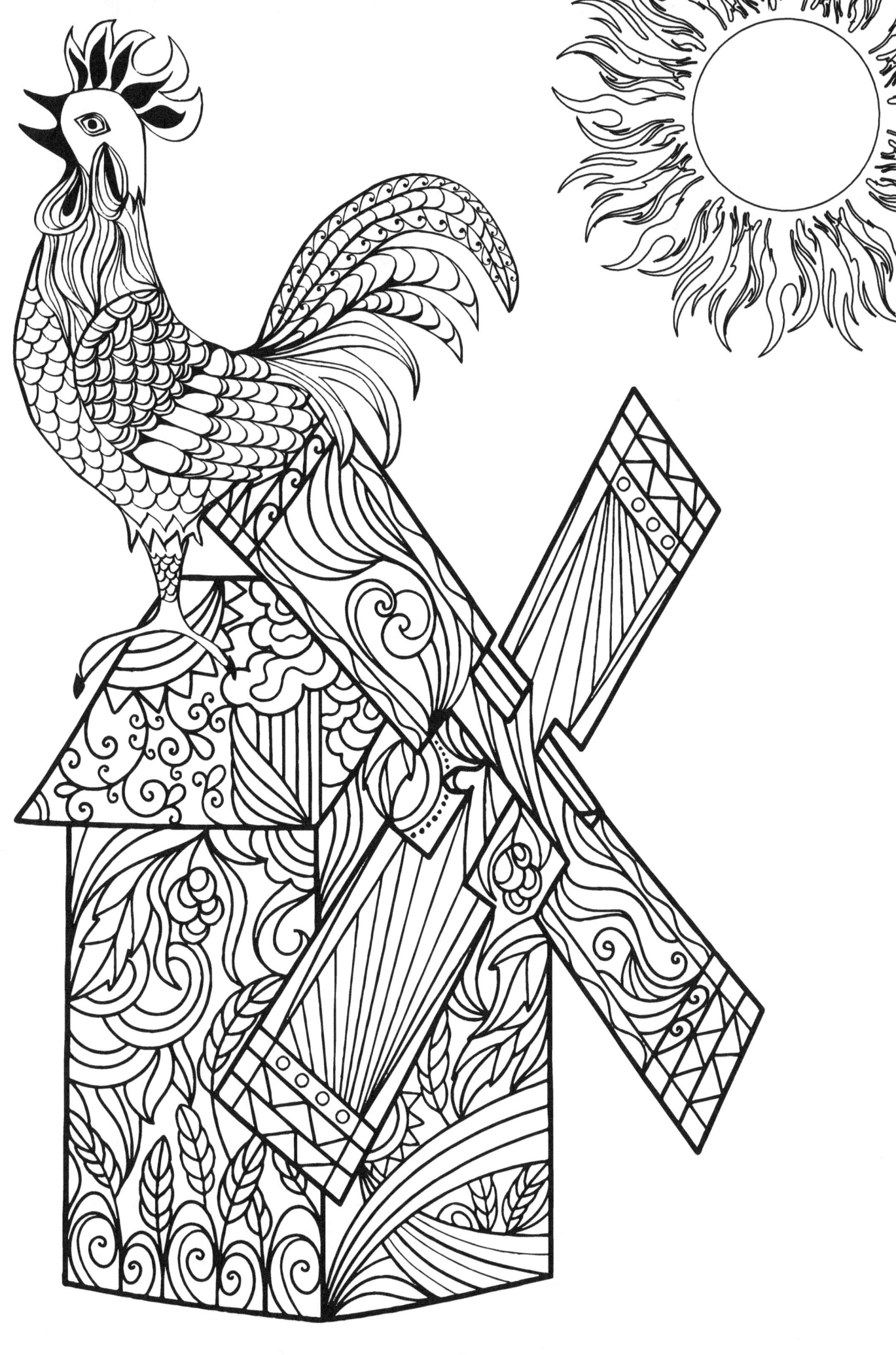

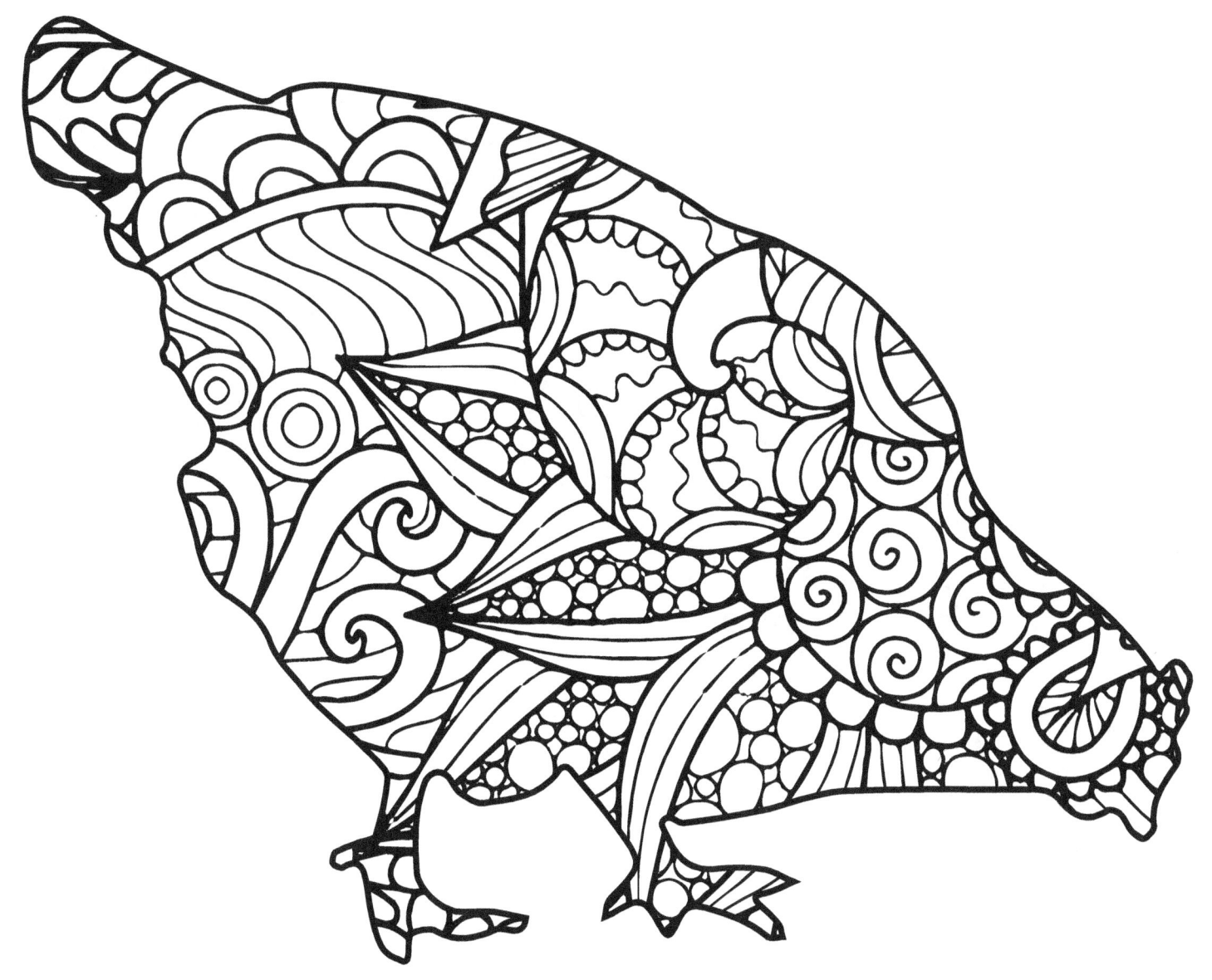

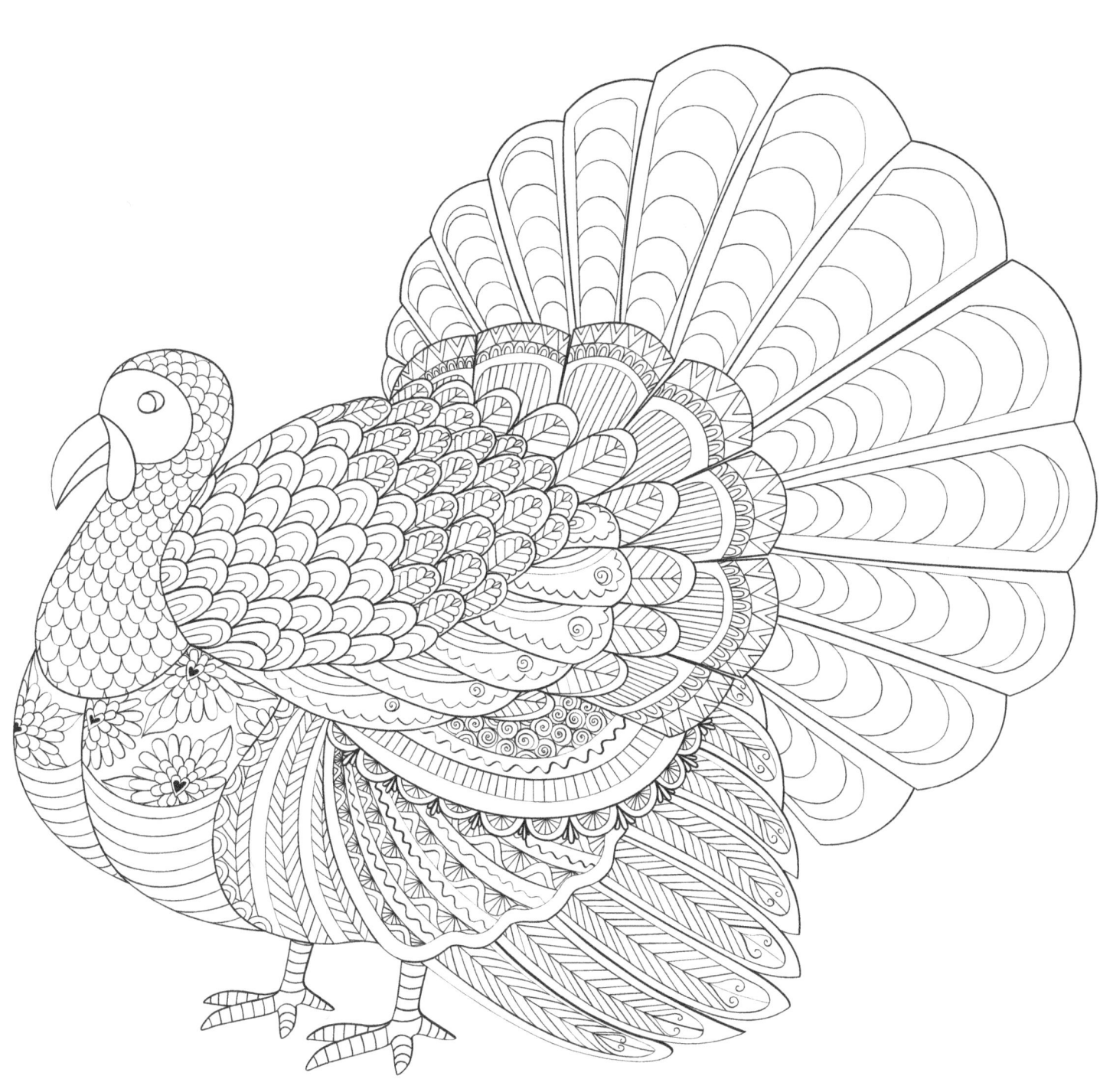

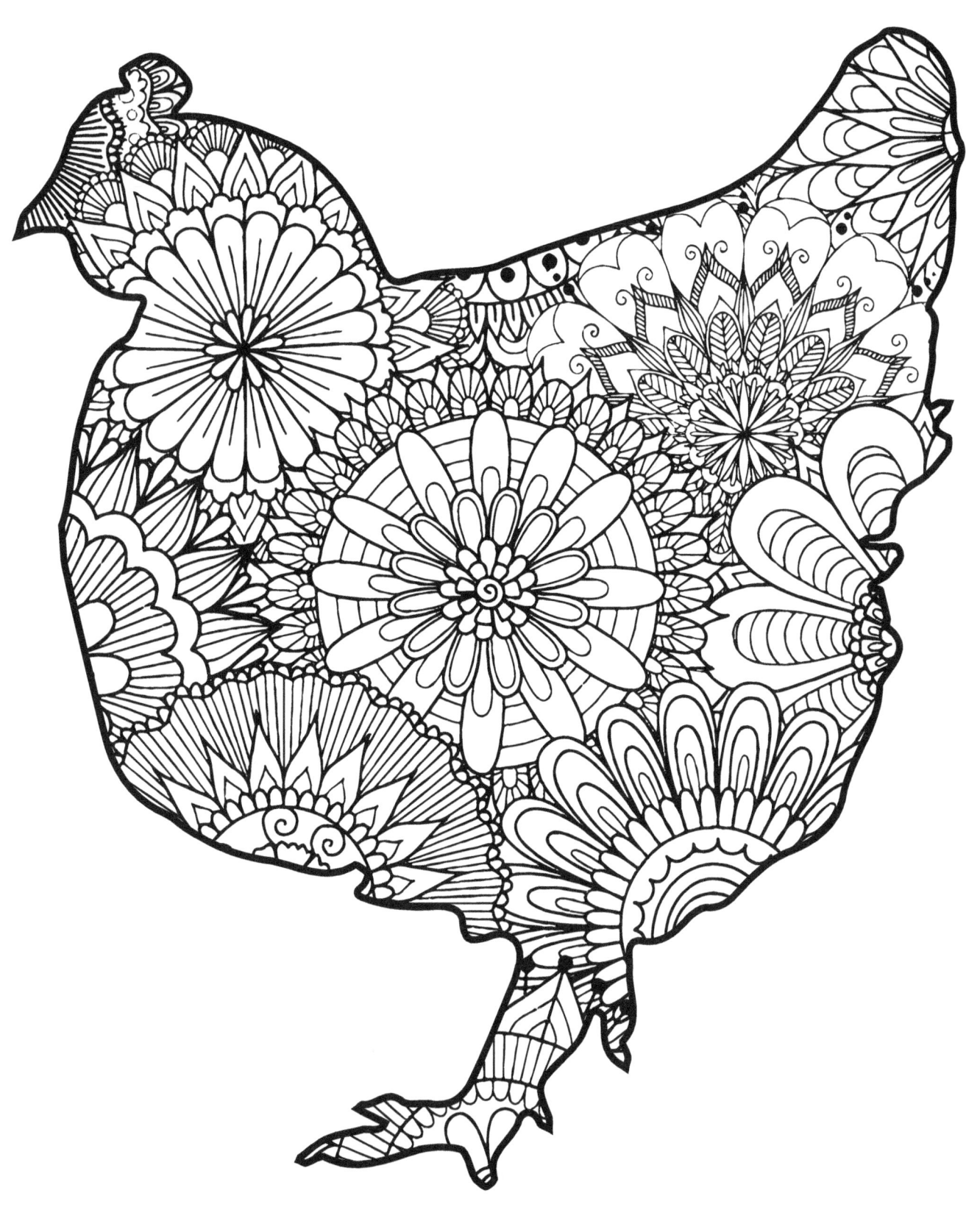

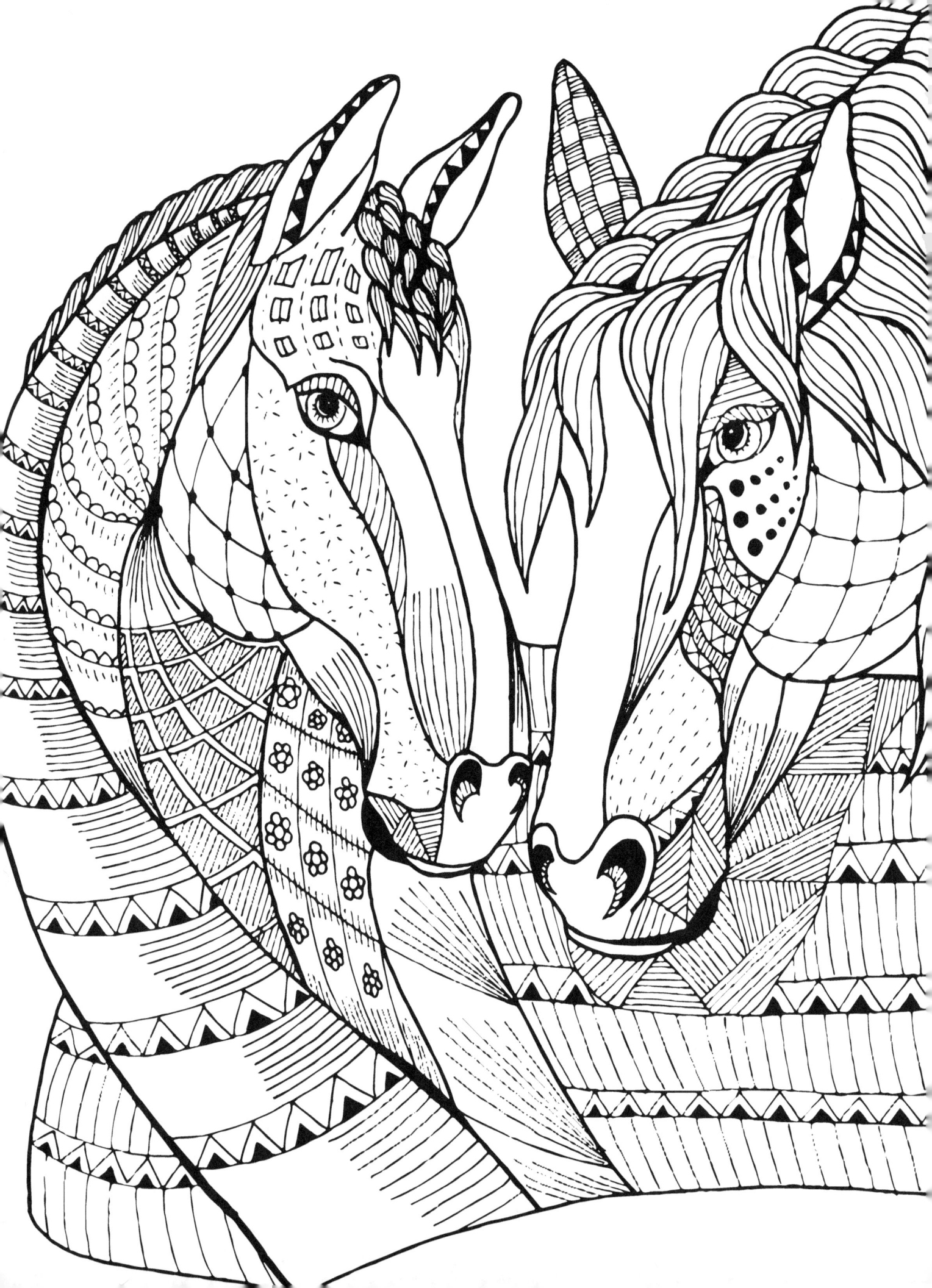

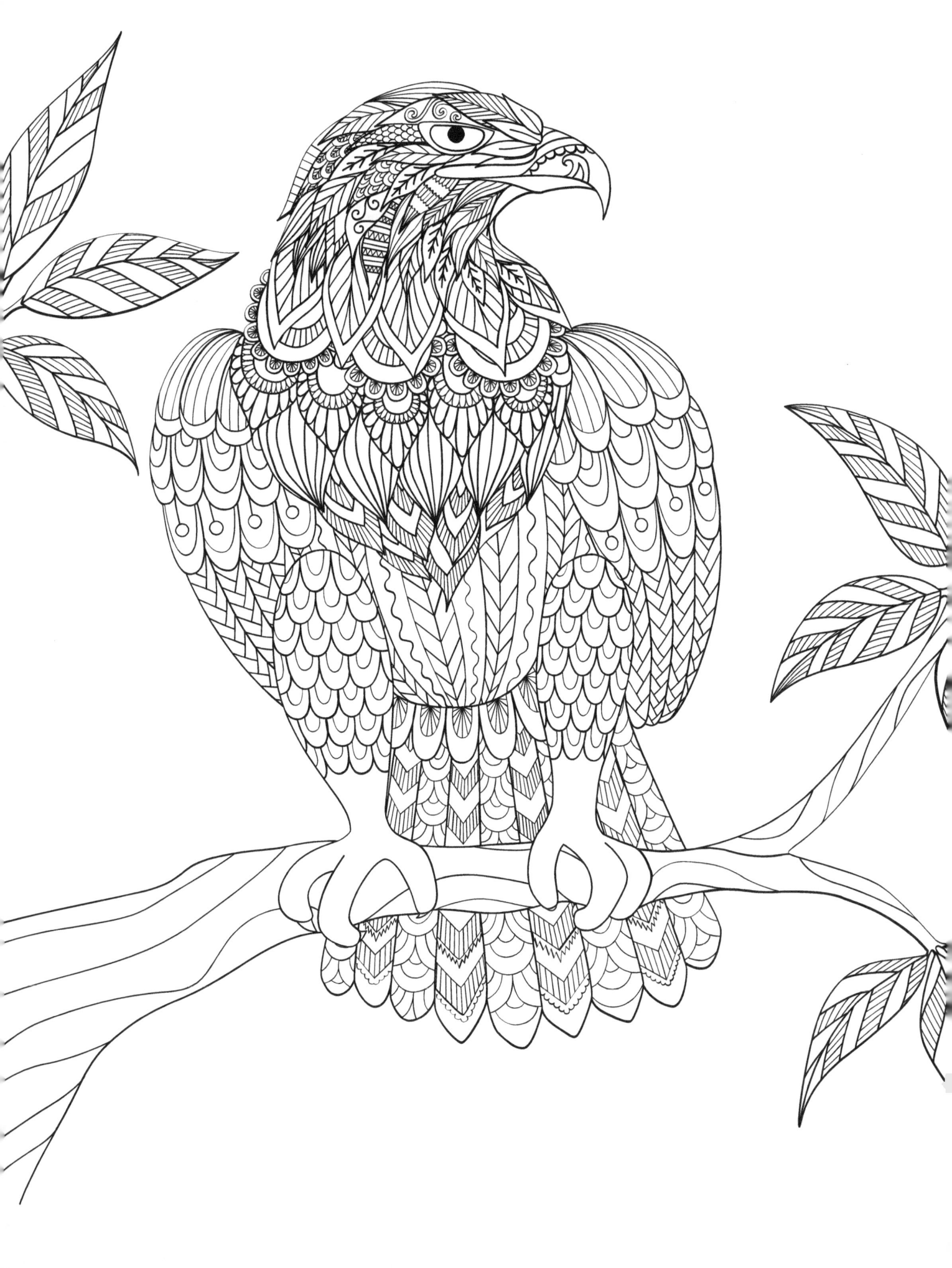

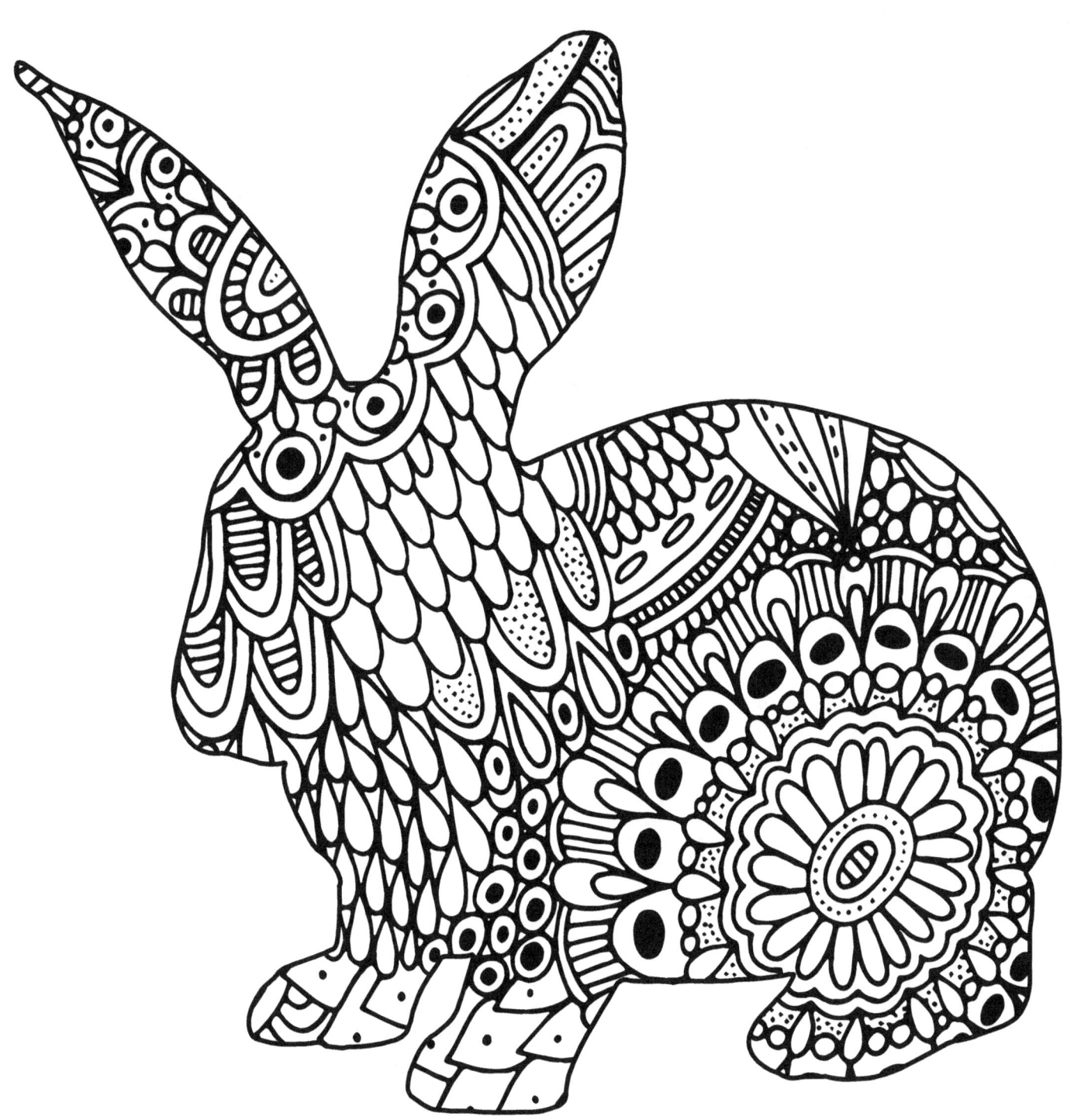

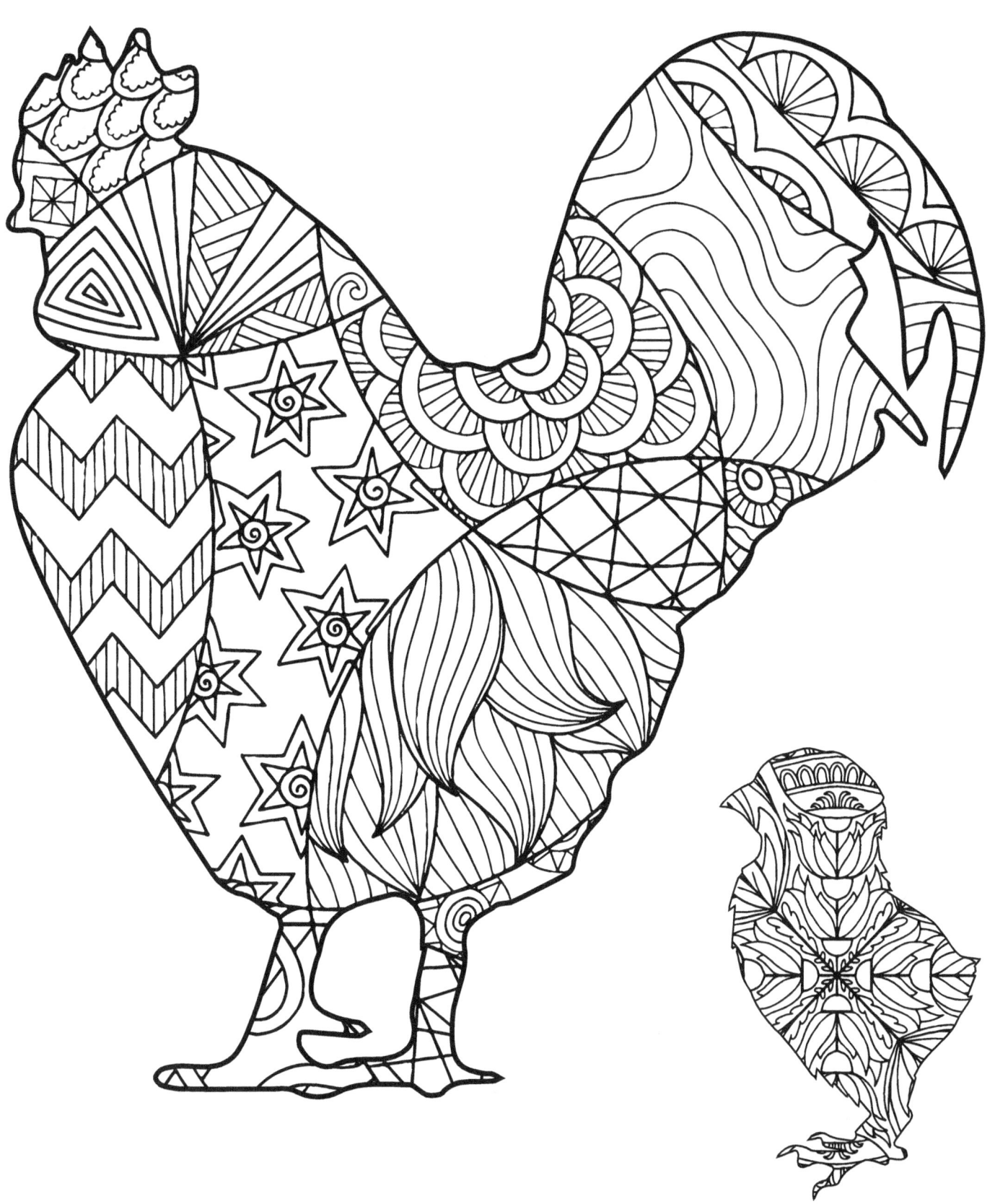

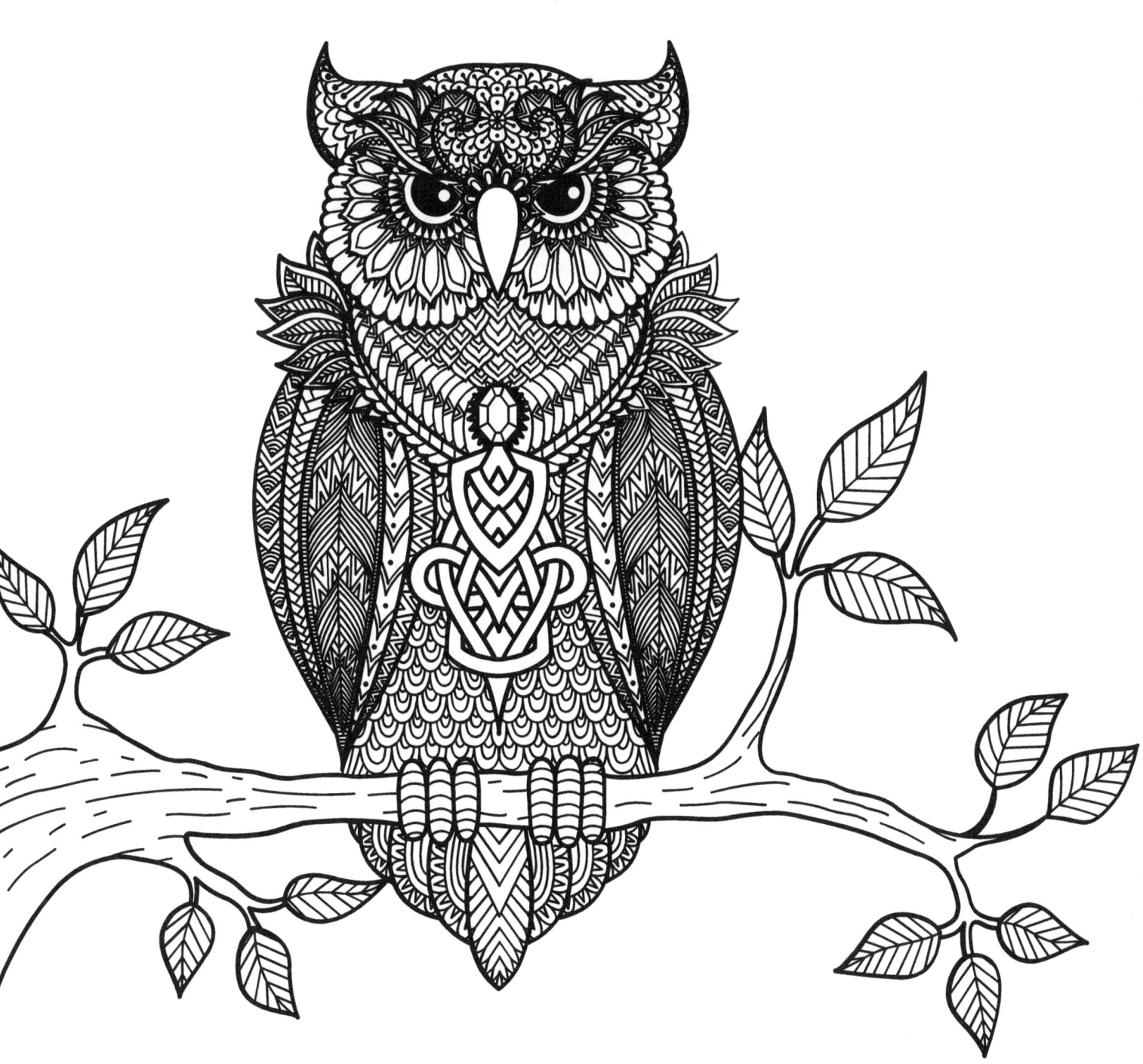

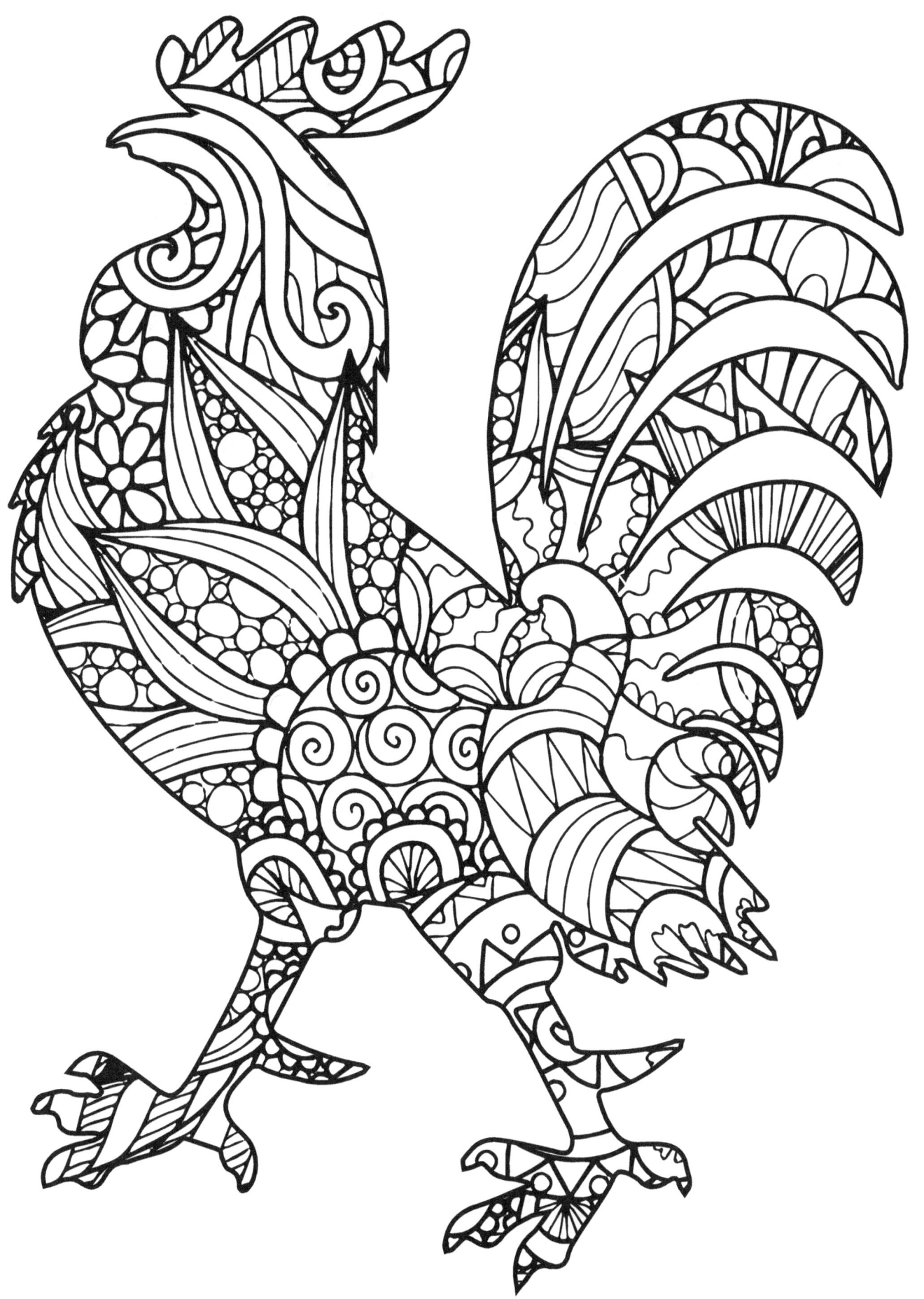

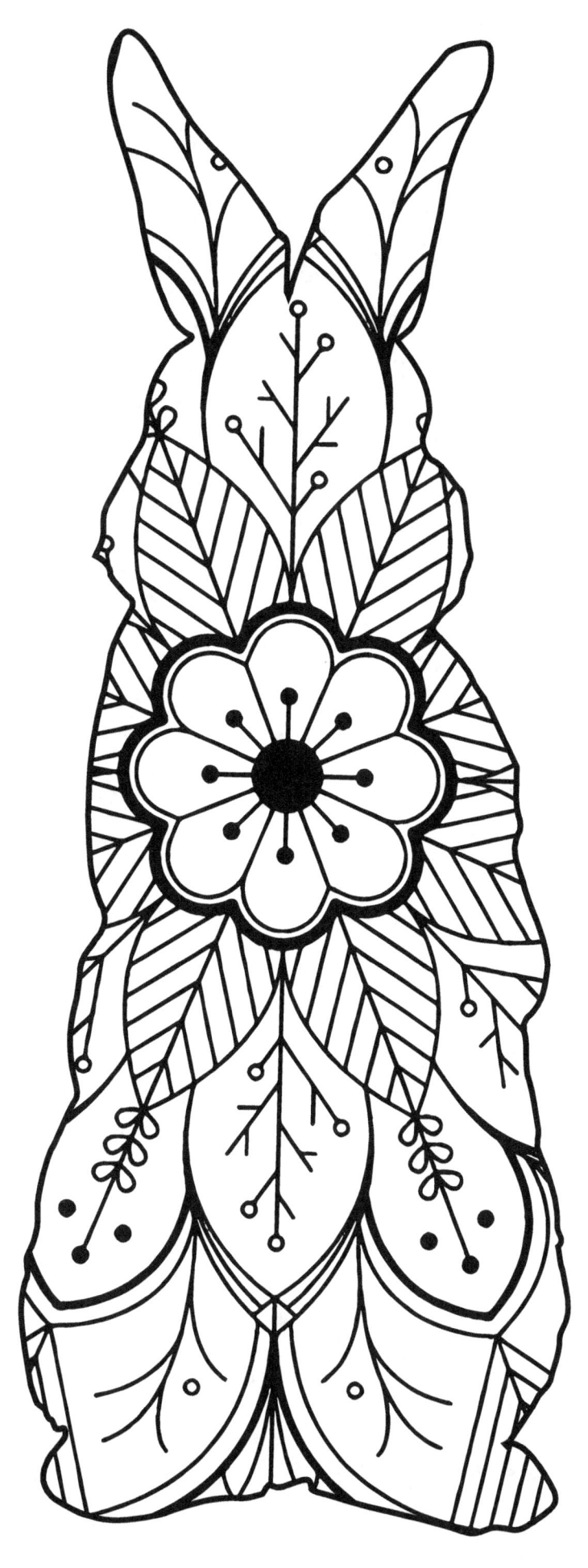

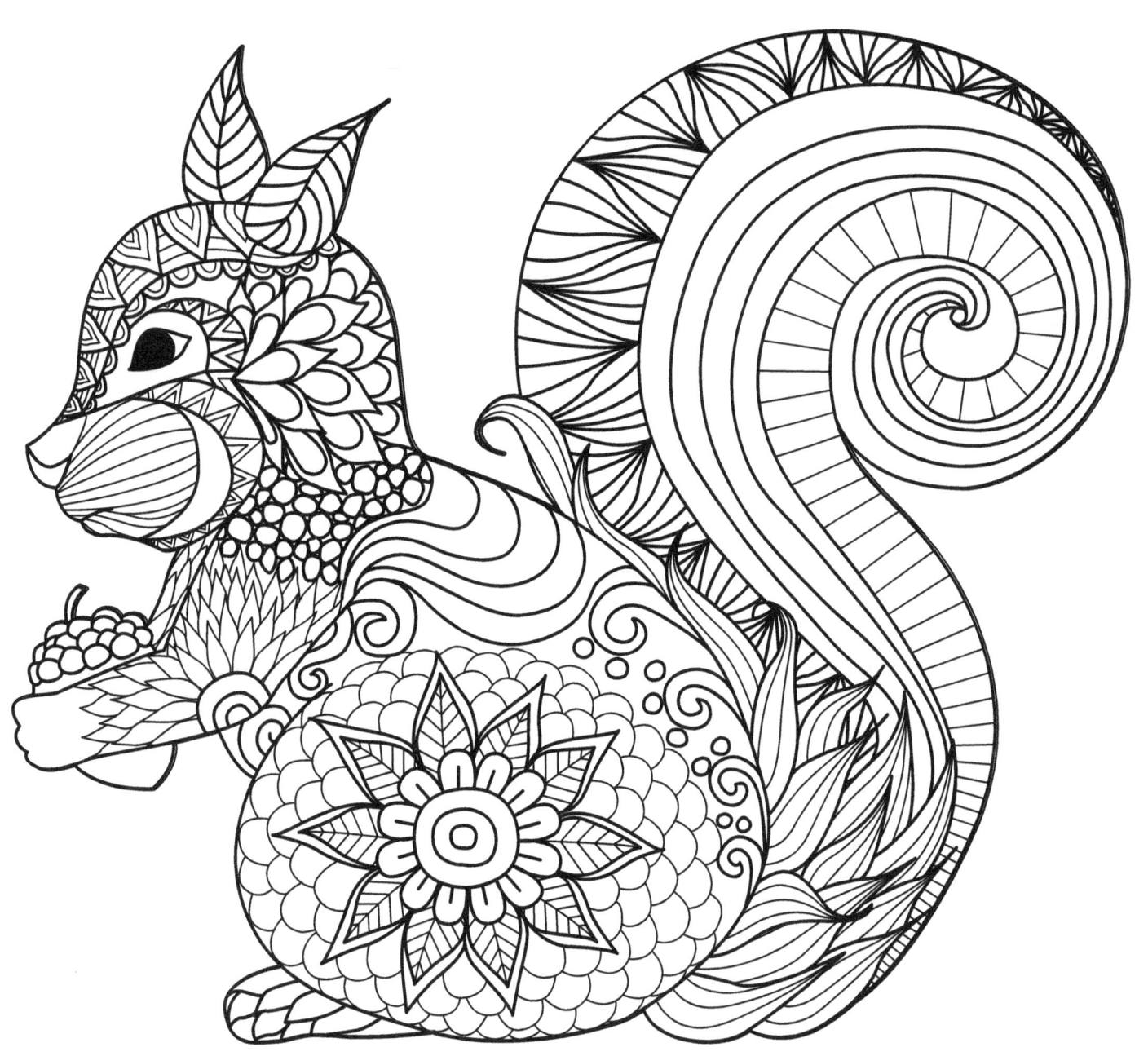

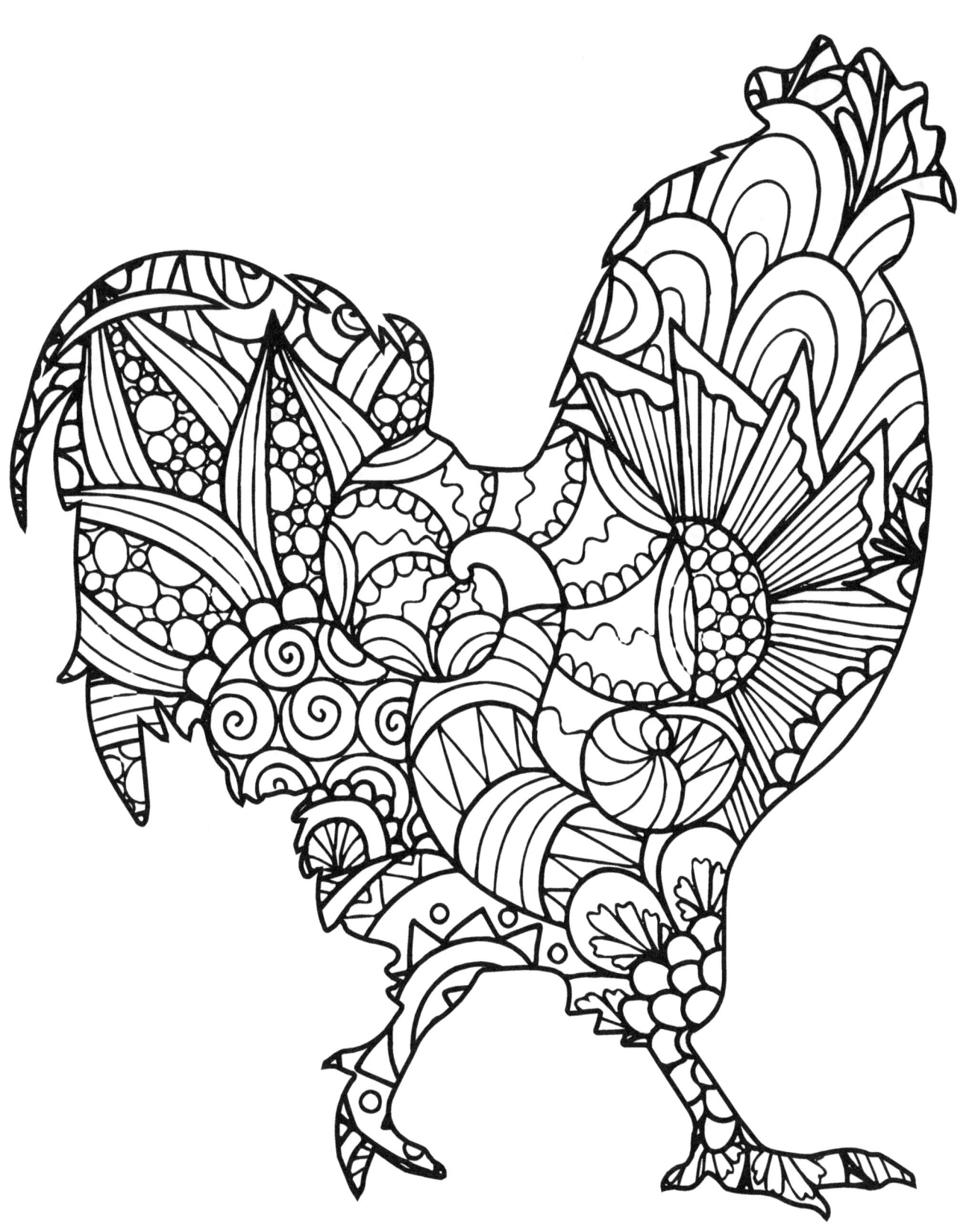